AF261116

Looking

for

Will

My Bardic Quest with Shakespeare

Greg Bell

Front Cover Artwork by Tim Marrs

Front Cover Design by Rain Livengood

Graphic Design/Layout by Rain Livengood and Greg Bell

Library of Congress

ISBN 978-1514345924

Second Edition 2015

Ion Drive Publishing

IonDrivePublishing.com

Table of Contents

Acknowledgments:

My thanks go to editors of *Buck & Mug* and *Tydes*, where versions of the following poems appeared: "Dance of Endings & Beginnings" and "Petty Tyrant."

My profound gratitude to all who have informed my quest for Shakespeare and touched *Alms for Oblivion*, particularly Kevin Brown, DJ Carlile, Luisa Puig, Phyllis Patterson, Neil Hudner, Diana Young, Rick Smith, Melodee Spevak, Kerri Dillon, John Mattson, Linda Abrams, Sarah Douglas, Beryl Sainsbury, Roger Thompson, Paul Sullivan, Jerry Rowitch, Richard Stone, Howard Sherman, Charm Lauritzen, Tom Bradac & Robin Smart, the Beadle of Stratford-on Avon.

Enormous thanks, too, to Ion Drive Publishing, to R. Merlin for his invitation to publish and for dragging me back into Faire, to Rain Livengood for his marvelous book layout and patience with my incessant edits, and to Tim Marrs for his fabulous design of the book cover, and to Nicky at the Shakespeare Birthplace Trust, who put me in touch with Tim.

Abundant love to my family, without whom I doubt I would have survived: Annette Bell, Alexis & Jim Gray, Jeannie Rao, Hope Alexander &. Ivan (Spiderman) Alexander, who 'scared away those bugs!'

Preface

Of late, I've been in a spelunking frame of mind. This likely has its origin in a hospital stay five years ago that had me dancing on the thinnest of fraying threads, poised at the doorway to the Undiscovered Country. No kidding, the docs didn't expect me to survive and told friends & family as much.

Around that time, when I returned from a float in the ethers, I had a conversation with myself: one self (higher self? witness?) asked the other self (lower self? ego?) *So, how do you feel about dying?* T'other self – startled to be so addressed, and inclined to be a bit huffy – settled down a bit and considered options: *Well, I'm in the ICU, tubes in every orifice (some never intended by nature.) Guess it's down to that.* I was facing the big Finger o'Fate; the options were purely ontological: To Be or Not To Be! So Self #2 came up with a plan: *I could do it! If I have to, I could do it! But if I do, I want to be alert to enjoy the ride!* That's when I (we?) decided that, while the drugs (among others, morphine) they were pumping into me were pretty psychedelic, they kept me from the state of alert I wanted to possess to be awake to the Grand Journey. After a while, Self #1 responded, *You've still got work to do. Better buck up, boyo!* Guess I did.

So this is me, 'bucking up' & doing (some of) the work. I want to thank R. Merlin (Myrrhlyn to me and, henceforth, ever so) for helping me do it. When we reconnected after my little 5 month stay in Hospital Hell, he invited me to consider an offer to publish. I stalled, thinking my next project had to be a book about my experience (called **A Second Life**, by the way, in case you're interested.) That project, however, languishes in the doldrums of the week or so of which I have only the dimmest recollection. (I'm soon to go into hypnotherapy for that...)

Meanwhile, Myrrhlyn has enticed me back to my old family, the world of Faire, where once I dove into the unfathomable pool of William Shakespeare, "deeper than did ever plummet sound."[1]

Shakespeare

Dear Voyager, venture back in time with me to English Lit, Jesuit H.S., El Paso, Texas, where Mr. LaChapelle has instructed us to turn to *Julius Caesar*. A reverential hush fills the classroom, (or was it dread?), as I evaluate the image of the Bard and think, *Gee, what a funny lookin' guy; sure glad I don't look like him!* If only I had known...

I will tell you now that when, for the first time, I swept aside the burlap behind the Main Stage in Agoura and stepped into the world of Faire through Shakespeare, I had a startling realization: no matter how well prepared I was, no matter who I thought I was, no matter how I handled myself, I would <u>never</u> live up to filling the biggest shoes in the known universe! NOBODY could! Somehow, once I got over the shock, that realization freed me to do my best.

I was off on a quest for the Bard! I just tallied my experience in playing Shakespearean leads, and I've arrived at 5. *Henry V* gains pre-eminence, as, just out of UCLA, I garnered the role at Marin Shakespeare Festival. (I recall, when offstage and listening to the oratory of the Chorus, thinking how fantastic it was, and how, one day, I'd like a crack at it. Got my chance at Shakespeare in the Park, Fort Worth, TX, in 1998. Chorus doesn't count as a lead, though.) So, while I've also played Cyrano & other wonderful roles, nothing has compared to the power and complexity of the Shakespearean lead. That said, how does one compare a single offspring of that kind of sire with the sire himself? Impossible.

So I attempted the impossible, determined to make it a rich experience for all, myself included. I can only hope that in some small way I succeeded. Thus the spelunking, as I dig through winding caves of the past.

The enclosed is a chronicle of my journey with the Bard of Avon—inextricably interwoven with my experience at Faire. In fact, my first exposure to Faire was at Blackpoint in the summer of '71, when I was performing Henry V, fresh out of college and wet behind the ears. My director, Mark Bramhall, insisted I do no side gigs, to keep my focus on Hank Cinque, but I attached myself to a Commedia troupe emerging from the Shakespeare festival, headed by Ugo Baldessari, with Janie Atkins & Jim Mairs as the young lovers, Paul Willis as Pantalone. Peter Kors was there, and I think Bob Feero and Dan Caldwell. (Ah! bittersweet memories, those...) Hope Alexander (who was later to become my wife) was there, with Max Klein as Caliban on a leash. I was enthralled. It was the beginning of many a trip in "the Time Tunnel of the High & Low" (thanks, Myrrhlyn, for the phrase) that is Faire.

So here's to our experiences together, and to their resurrection in remembrance!

The Bard Card

Some time in the latter years of the 20th Century, a cloud parted and bestowed on me what I can only describe as a kind of artificial fame. It was likely 1988. I'd been playing Shakespeare at Faire for the past few years, and I got a call from Melodee Spevack: 'Did I have any pics of myself as Shakespeare?' So happens, I did, as I'd been engaged by Rick Smith @ Central Coast Renaissance Faire to appear as a primary theme character, and he'd taken the trouble to get a studio picture taken. (The gig was a great pleasure!) Well,

Melodee, whom I'd known from Southern Faire as a fetching Red Sonja in leathern bikini and baldric packed with a sword, said she knew a guy (John Naulin) who'd received a call from folk in England who wanted to create a holographic likeness of Shakespeare for what they later called The Bard Card, and he was looking for a model.

She said she'd be by after fighter practice—yes, she really could sling that thing!—to pick up the pic after 11:00 PM. Who am I to argue with a woman with a sword? So she came by, we shared a bit of sherry, she took the picture with her, and the rest, as they say, is history: Someone faxed it to England, they said 'Yes,' and I was instructed to show up at such 'n such a time at a Simi Valley studio, where together we created the holographic image of Shakespeare that was to cause such a stir as to create my fifteen minutes of notoriety.

The Authorship 'Controversy'

Meanwhile, playing the Bard over time at Faire, I became acquainted with some of the theories of authorship that abound to this day—no matter how improbable! As you may imagine, I developed an interest. I recall a visit to Elysium, a nudist camp in Topanga Canyon. I'd never been there before, in the altogether among strangers. As it happened, I ran into a fellow I knew, who greeted me and exchanged pleasantries. There we were, willies dangling, when he asked what it was I held in my hand. It was a pamphlet I'd bought at the Bacon library in Pasadena in my quest of the Real Will, written by Delia Bacon, attributing authorship of the Shakespearean canon to—wait for it!—Sir Francis Bacon. Well, my friend leaned in and said, "You know who <u>really</u> wrote Shakespeare?" "Pray tell," said I.

He began to glow, suffused, I supposed, with some insider knowledge: "It was a convocation of Ascended Masters, who, on their return to this mortal plane, had collaborated on the work: Bacon, Marlowe, Jonson, Raleigh, the Earl of Oxford and the Queen herself!"

I went off to sun my altogether...

The Play's the Thing

The idea for a play was something Kevin Brown & I cooked up from gigging together. (He's the guy who hired me.) Kevin had me and Luisa Puig (the queen) to dinner for a planning session for something like *Shakespeare & Elizabeth*, which I was to write, she, of course to play QE 1, Kevin to cover multiple roles. Soon thereafter, she moved to the Bay Area, Kevin ever engaged with the Imagineers and Faire. For multiple reasons, that triumvirate was not to be.

Still, I was determined to write—and ferret out the truth. *Did Shakespeare write Shakespeare?* My quest inevitably led me to the conclusion he must have, though it was all the rage then to attribute authorship to someone else. This got my goat. Imagine WS, lazing about in the Elysium of olde with Anais Nin, when Robert Green saunters up and says, "Hey, Will, they say that pipsqeak Oxford wrote your stuff!" Aroint!

Alms for Oblivion

Thus was born the impulse to write *Alms for Oblivion*, which was to address the authorship question and connect the dots about how such achievements by Shakespeare might have been possible. I will unequivocally say that *Alms* would not have been possible without my experience of Faire, providing an enormously rich & paradoxical context of Living History: from a greater understanding of how the Lord Chamberlain's Players gave WS the home base he needed for his extraordinary accomplishments, to a superabundance of Temptations about, that gave me a (forgive me) hands-on experience of the Dark Lady. The contrast abounds:

Anglican mass via the 1552 Book of Common Prayer after Cock & Feathers, the night before.

Past Times with Good Company

Still, something eluded me: I had to get to England, breathe the air, touch the stone. That became possible when John Mattson, the talented musician who'd served as band leader for the production of **Taming of the Shrew** I'd produced & directed for Faire (and THAT's another story!) recruited me to join the group Pastimes with Good Company, headed by Linda Abrams, for a living history tour of England. The universe was co-operating!

On the tour, we all sang & danced, rubbing up against one another as people on tour will do, and played a variety of roles. Among others, I took on the architect-builder of Montacute House in Somerset, the master of Speke Hall near Liverpool (a hideout for Jesuits), and the young Will at Hoghton Tower, Lancashire. I was in living history heaven.

But it gets better. After the tour, I stayed on, first in London where I visited the British Museum. Once I'd torn myself away from the Elgin Marbles, I made my way to the research library, where they were kind enough to allow me into the reading rotunda for antiquities, despite the fact I'd no letter of introduction from university. You may imagine my thrill on finding the 16th Century Latin lesson plan by Erasmus, or the joy of handling the heavy tome of Golding's translation of Ovid's *Metamorphoses* that Shakespeare might very well have touched! I was on track.

On the way out, feeling certain I'd gotten what I needed from the library, my attention fell on an exhibition of illuminations. Once I'd finished admiring the fabulous Book of Kells, done in brilliant paints & inks that seemed never to have faded (no wonder—they'd used precious gems & gold,) I came on a collection of antique letters penned by famous persons.

Most of the letters were illegible to me, but one struck me both for its clarity and its haunting content: it was penned by the young Elizabeth Tudor to her brother, Edward VI, the young king who was under the thumb of his regent, who actually held the reins of governance. Mary & Elizabeth were older than Edward but had been bypassed for the male heir. In this letter she expressed concern for his health that seemed absolutely authentic, but, hovering in the background, there seemed to be the intimation she and Mary would be bypassed (of course!) in the succession by Edward and his regent for Lady Jane Grey (however briefly.) Then, too, the fate of her mother, Anne Boleyn, seemed also to hover...

Shakespeare Country

But on to Shakespeare Country and Stratford-on-Avon, where I stayed with a woman whose daughter, Sarah Douglas, I'd met in L. A. 2 weeks before leaving for England. She had said, "You must stay with my mother. She's practically the mayor of Stratford!" Doors opened everywhere.

Sarah's ex-brother-in-law, Roger Thompson, who owned and managed Guide Friday, arranged for me to have full & free access to all the usual Shakespeare sites: the Birthplace House on Henley Street, Mary Hathaway's home & Shakespeare's mother's family estate, Arden House. I was absorbing it into my bones, but the best was yet to come.

The Town Beadle

One Sunday I passed by the Guild Chapel whose interior murals of suffering souls had also suffered whitewashing by the Protestant regime of Shakespeare's day as too papist. I'd often been by, but it was always closed. Not today.

I wandered in, bent on viewing the murals some devoted soul had undertaken to restore. Up walked a bear of a man, barrel chested, beard bursting from his face, to address me with gusto in booming voice, "Are you here for the service, sir?"

"Ummm.... I *could* be..."

"Well, see here, we need a man to read the deacon's part. I'd do it, but I'm on the organ. Would you be so kind?" I looked to my left at the half dozen septuagenarian women, and he responded to my look, "Has to be a man!"

Same olde England, where girls were denied public education, and the aristocracy was loath to be ruled by a Queen. But I remained to read for the tiny congregation in ancient chapel.

Afterward, the jolly bear approached to thank me. He introduced himself as Town Beadle Robin Smart and offered me a bit of hospitality. He'd bicycled to the Guild for the service to which his office of Beadle had bound him. In deference to me and to ease conversation, he walked his bicycle beside as he escorted me to his home, a modest but delightful place, where he briefly introduced me to his wife, Ann, then made a couple ham sandwiches and offered me a Guinness. It was his last, so he made do with a can of bitters.

I noted the lovely grandfather clock of mulberry in his den, and he pointed out its provenance: the mulberry tree said to be planted by WS, cut from the gardens at New Place by the 18th Century Rev. Gastrell, annoyed by Bardolaters. (I used that!) Robin invited me to an outdoor production of *As You Like It* which he had to review for the local paper. I am dismayed to observe to you that the English, too, can do Shakespeare poorly.

My Gentle Pucke

After a wet, chilly June in England, July had turned hot and tawny. Beryl, Sarah's mother, ran a sweet shop on Church Street, and, for the first time, asked me for help. Of course, I'd help! I'd seen the lads of the nearby Edward VI Grammar School, the schoolroom of Shakespeare's youth, and it was emphatically NOT a tourist site. Here they were again, trying to cool down, ties loose, blazers off, cherub-cheeked, buying sodas & sweets, and somehow I gleaned that it was the final day of school. Aroint & Carpe Diem!

I got leave from Beryl and rushed up the street to the schoolhouse, built 1553, which sits above the Guild Hall where Shakespeare's father had once paid the players in his duty as Bailiff. As I arrived at the gate I observed a white-haired gent, doubtless the schoolmaster, pant leg tucked into his sock, wheeling a rickety bicycle, about to clasp the lock through the chains of the gate. I stopped him, expressed a profound desire to visit the schoolroom of Shakespeare's youth, as he stood there and smiled. (Doubtless he'd seen his share of Bardolaters...) While he wasn't about to un-finalize his closing ritual of the school year, he directed me to another entrance, where, he said, I could find the caretaker. I thanked him profusely and wished him a pleasant ride.

When I found the amiable Paul Sullivan he was engaged in a task that would take him 20-30 minutes, and he could not leave the room unlocked, so that, if he were to let me in, he'd have to lock me in the room until his return. Oh, darn!

He walked me to the room, reached for his iron ring of keys, unlocked and opened the doorway to my temple, my Holy of Holies. Hot, no doubt, the windows were closed, and it was a steambath, but no matter. He checked again with me.

I was sure. He closed the door and locked me in.

There I stood, in awe. I observed the room. Everywhere, but
especially above, were massive timbers that followed the
grain of the wood, which meant that, with the exception of
the blackboard, there was not a straight line in the place.

As with ancient cathedrals where passage over centuries has
worn dips in the stone floors and steps, so, too, the scuffling of
young feet had unevenly worn the floor into a wooden sea.
Adrift on that sea, I was dizzy, had to sit and gather myself, so
I sat beside the leaded windows, where I observed the room
for a while, then slipped into reverie.

It was the clank of keys turning the lock that brought me back.
The groundsman apologized for the delay, remarking on the
heat. I hadn't noticed. "Ah, ye'r sittin' in his seat, are ye!" He
pointed out the plaque to my left, denoting tradition that
young Will was reputed to have sat there.

You may believe I bought Paul a pint or two. Or three.

The Readiness is All!

I carried a treasure trove of facts, impressions & inspiration
with me back to L. A., where I tried to make sense of it all.
Dr. Jerry Rowitch gave me my first venue at the Venice
Sculpture Gardens on Abbott Kinney Blvd, but the play would
metamorphose over time, expanding and contracting.
Richard Stone helped me into the Crystal Theater, where
Howard Sherman saw an early version and took it on as
director—as well as dramaturg. We joked that we were
leaving "dead babies by the roadside," the children of my pen
who had to be cut. May they rest in peace.

It was daunting to write *Alms*, and even more daunting to perform: a two act, two hour play, with no one to share the load on stage!   After each performance I felt I'd run a marathon. I kept it up for 8 years, self-producing locally and playing paid gigs around the country, from The Itchy Foot Cabaret in the shadow of the Music Center to the University of Hawai'i to Brigham Young University, to the Edinburgh Fringe Festival. Ironically, it took a gig @ Shakespeare Orange County under Tom Bradac to finally get the L. A. Times to review the show. It was glowing.

But it was late. After gigs @ Palmdale Playhouse, produced by Dea McAllister, and then Ohlone College, I came to the realization that, to make a go of it and draw the requisite audience numbers, I needed the 'TVQ' I'd not achieved, so, when I reached the age at which the Bard of Avon passed away, I let pursuit of the Bard pass away from my endeavors.

The Past is Prologue

Still, something extraordinary happened in the quest, the weaving of this tapestry. It's that experience I hope to pass on to you, Gentle Reader, with this heartfelt wish: may whatever harvest you reap from my humble effort serve to bring us all closer to an embrace of the daunting paradox of the human condition, from "The weight of this sad time we must obey, Speak what we feel, not what we ought to say"[2] to "We are such stuff as dreams are made on, and our little life is rounded with a sleep."[3]

[1] - Prospero, *The Tempest*
[2] - Edmond, *King Lear*
[3] - Prospero

Soul of the Age!
The applause, delight, the wonder of our stage
My Shakespeare, rise!
Ben Jonson

But all our wants by wit may be supply'd,
And art makes up what fortune has deny'd
Ovid, *Metamorphoses*

... I have seen the hungry ocean gain
Advantage on the kingdom of the shore
And the firm soil win of the watery main,
Increasing store with loss, and loss with store...
Sonnet 64

And yet to times in hope my verse shall stand
Praising thy worth, despite his cruel hand.
Sonnet 60

My comfort is that old age, that ill layer-up
of beauty, can do no more spoil upon my face.
Henry V

To the Bard himself, who never failed to inspire my quest
To my son, Michael, who had to grow up as Hamnet
And to all who encouraged me & all who thought me mad

The Earth Corroborates My Find

Stranger in town, I am alone
as I leave the Harvard COOP
(rabbit warren of books, books, books)
pleased with myself and with my find,
for under my arm is a hard cover edition
impeccably edited by G.B. Harrison
of The Complete Works of Shakespeare.

As I trudge through Harvard Square
my feet crunch and sink through the outer
crust of snow, frozen thread from sky
to earth that sucks at me as mud,
but winter's chill on my bones is overcome
by the warmth of this my find,
for all but the apocryphal plays
are now at my fingertips,
destined to be well marked and thumbed
in my Shakespearean peregrinations:

From *The Comedy of Errors*
through the Henries and the Richards
to the sublime valedictory
of *The Tempest*, all here!
All here *Venus and Adonis*,
The Rape of Lucrece,
the cryptic, enigmatical
Phoenix and the Turtle
and the Sonnets, open windows
to the Bard himself
all of whom I feel I've freed

These many lives I carry with me
lost in this realization, when
a bird chirps my senses back
to the moment – such a moment!
aware now for the first time
the sun is peeking through
winter's miasma, melting icicles
evanescent on the trees, revealing tiny
mighty green buds a'growin'
and up through the snow

crocus pushes toward the sky
for it's now halleluiah spring
and we join the chorus, ghosts and I
as my leaping heart begins to sing

Faire Song

Welcome stranger, friend, unto our shire,
This goodly glade wherein we play our faire,
And fairly play, we trust, that you'll admire
The Pageantry unfurled before you here.
For herein do we raise our cups in cheer
To Celebrate the Sacred Rites of Spring,
To toast the coming bounty of the year,
To let each bell and heart with laughter ring!

So tumble in and gaze upon array
Of breeze-flung banners, colours' riotous dance,
The lads and winsome lasses who hold sway
With beauty that's for aye and aye Romance.
The Queen brings revel music for the May;
We trust you'll have a jollity today!

Petty Tyrant

How oft have I entreat the petty tyrant
Of the turning world to slow his course,
Be not a brittle, clicking clock, but pliant
To the moment's breath, to beauty's force.
Yet still the summer's fragile flower fades,
The stars perforce continue in their tracks,
The whilst we cry against the coming shades
And lose our purchase on the shaded facts:
For as the laboured climb to mountain's peak
Exacts the greater effort, stretching Time,
Or as the headlong plunge from aerie steepe
Cuts down the screaming hour in his prime –
    More, still, do we, in tragi-comic rite,
    Turn back the clock, confounding Time his might!

Close Encounters

In the 70's, I used to show up in Agoura in tights (or billowy pants)
and a turban. I would wander around faire, observing everything
and feasting on sights & sounds. Occasionally, I'd run into
someone who interested me: winsome lasses, to be sure, but ladies
with lovely children, or couples, young or old, in love, perhaps
someone in a funk– someone I wished to engage. I would
approach them as if to speak, but nothing would come out. I'd
shake my head in sorrow, touch my throat by way of explanation,
reach for a piece of paper in my pouch and show it to them. It read:

Fair Lady, Kind Sir–

My gentle Poet's tongue has been beguiled
by the fiendish curse of a fearsome sorcerer.

Yet rejoice! The pow'r to break this spell
this very moment lies within your will:
If you but press my palm with a paltry piece
of silver (the folding coinage of the realm
is known to work as well or even better)
you will free my Muse
that I may speak for thy Pleasure
beauteous Poetry!

I've locked within this treasure vault
the wisdom of Kabir,
then there's the lovely Rubaiyat
of old Khayam to hear.

But if in English verse you would prefer
to put me to the test
there are the sonnets of Shakespeare–
which one do you love best?

(should cash become an issue
– for the right winsome lass:)

If gold or silver hast thou none,
Fear not, gentle miss.
This fearsome curse may be undone
with but a maiden's kiss!

If, on any account, they opted to proceed, I determined to make it
worth their while and held forth (from memory) on the poet of
their choice. I grew to love the intimacy of sharing this glorious
poetry with these people, and, to this day, people approach me to
tell me how much that encounter meant to them, their spouse or
children. Meant a lot to me, too.

This was the formative experience that gave me the template for my
approach to filling the biggest shoes I'd ever have to fill: those of
the genius bard, William Shakespeare. It became all about sharing
the quiet intimacy of the Bard's most personal work, his sonnets.

They might press my palm with a bit more cash afterwards,
and we'd be done. I'm still in touch with a gentleman I met
there with his now deceased wife— Aannd occasionally, a kiss would
lead to other adventures. But that was the 70's, dontcha know...

From the forge of this Faire experience, influenced by the exoticism
of Omar Khayam & the simple beauty of Kabir, new poems began to
emerge.

Where All Gates Meet

Seven days
of passing through
The Seven Gates of Dawn
and on the evening
of the seventh
falling belly low
through
the center of theEarththeEarththeEarth
to leap headlong
open-eyed
into the

Void

There is a longing
in my heart
growing shorter –
no not so
but opening wider
stretching longer
into the Circle Great
to shoot the gap
behind your eyes
and reach into infinity
through touching
other souls

Bridging
the
Gap

Coming down from yoga class
the yoga teacher-student
floats on over to the Pleasure Faire

to tickle the other end
of the continuum
and the apparent personality

diagnosed upon occasion
as an acute attempt
to bridge the schizophrenic gap

with Sweet Will's words
with Songs of Kabir and Khayyam
to the revelry of plumes & paints

the pouring stout and biting swords
the peacock feathers and the flesh
and the sweet intoxication in the air

to plant the seed of stillness
in this all too passing fancy

the desperate endeavor
for a temporary pleasure

Red 'n Ripe

O, 'tis wondrous strange 'n rare it is
how yesterday at Faire (of course)
I spied a magickal glorious sight

it was rainin' mist
in the middle of a sunlit day
it was rainin' banners 'n bosoms
red 'n ripe
it was rainin' torches in caves
'n clouds sittin' on steeples
'n ticklin' their bums
'n nobody mindin' it
in fact they was enjoyin' it
it was that kind o'day

'n I hafta laugh when I think
o' the smiles it was rainin' right an' left
(y'know the kinda silly grin
from earlobe to earlobe
that says ye just gave away
tha last farthin' worth o' chocolate
not becuz ye give a damn about no silly rules
but cause ye feel so happy 'n content
with what ye had ye jus' hafta share it
wi' someone)
'n every one o'them smiles
reminded me o' you

faith, lass, I saw ye
in little girls 'n old men
in mothers 'n little blue-eyed boys
I saw ye jumpin' out from
the elderberry bush behind
the oak wi' the toadstool
underneath

so just before I crazy goes
I sez I does, Why, yea!
'n joins ye in the bushes

My maiden voyage as William Shakespeare was @ the Ben Jonson
Restaurant, on the wharf in San Francisco, where I was hired as co-host,
 Ben Jonson (ca 1980.) This is a duty I shared with Michael Caweltie, but
one which proved to be problematic when he descended the staircase as I
regaled people from a table-top in the bar. "Ben," sez I. "Ben," he replies.

Afterwards, Michael, opined that I would make a fitting Shakespeare, as
he gently pointed out my receding hairline. I could nothing do but agree...

The sonnet below is the first I ever wrote, on a dare from the publisher of
San Francisco Magazine, whom I met there. As I retrieve the dimming
memory, he'd commented about SF: "It's the other side of heaven."
Well, I mostly agreed, though I confessed I found the prospect problematic,
but that I'd address it in a sonnet I would write on the subject.
"Yes," said he, "and I will publish it!" Well, then I just had to do it!

Contribution to a Tribute's Quandary
("San Francisco: It's the other side of heaven!")

And so you set me on to write a sonnet
For your pleasure (and mine own, Dear Sire,)
But more, I trust, a feather in the bonnet
Of a city that doth heights inspire:
With her beauteous sights, her windy passion,
Her voluptuous anatomy,
Bequeathing brisk caress in lover's fashion,
Or tickling hearts with tiny atomies,
O'er beckoning bridges, she, like naughty bride,
Through cloud and sun, the play of ice and fire,
Seduces folk to heaven's nearer side,
The place we fancy as our favorite shire—
But, of words we set on, (truth to tell!)
I reckon "heaven's other side" as... Well...?

Addendum: To this day, I still don't know whether he published it.

Sonnet for People Magazine*

In all the spinning world on which we tread
(Inhabitants by gravitation)
There is, methinks, an interwoven thread
Transcending ways or name or station:

We crane our necks to chart our history,
And in the vault of sky we find a spar
On which to hang our tales of destiny
Defined by that mere speck we name 'a star.'

A light, a self-illumined sun, 'tis called,
Fixed in its sphere to course the heavens bright,
Yet by the shooting star are we enthralled,
Bright flame, brief candle burning out the night!

But that these days Sweet Will endures 'tis well,
*Who would not praise that purposed not to sell.***

*My 15 minutes of fame, arising out of the then recent outing by journalists
in the UK that the model for their Bard Card was some upstart in Culver City,
California. My thanks again to Melodee Spevack, who rousted me for the gig.

**WS, from Sonnet 21:
Let them say more that like of hearsay well;
I will not praise that purpose not to sell.

Pastimes With Good Companie

Approach

In decompression
via iron bird
easing down
through clouds amarch
into Gatwick
gateway to the verdant
rain-drenched
sceptered isle

and somewhere in my heart
the strings of home are plucked
by invisible ancient hands

Circles of Sarum*

While away the minutes brief
turn them whirling to an hour
or two   a momentary timeless

amble into English countryside
beyond the rolling pasturelands
replete with ram & cow & crow
with blackbird, golden nuthatch
swallow   beyond them all to

the rivers' radiused confluence
      wheel of wonder
      hub of danger
      wheel of teeming

      in hypnotic flow

the circle of stone wings
      and point of departure

*Sarum is the original name for settlements in the area of Salisbury, located at the
confluence of 5 rivers: the Nadder, Ebble, Wylye and Bourne, tributary to the
Avon, at the edge of Salisbury Plain. Stonehenge is 11 miles to the North.

Druid Dance

At Arbor Low – my first exposure to a stone circle.
Stones were still, but the circle still turning.

We turn in the circle, turn in the dance
flung on the spinning wheel
weaving the tapestry as if by chance
seeking design as we reel

Reeling in darkness, reeling in light
none is the path but is curled
seasons of summer, seasons of night
whirling the way of the world

Prayer

O Will, sweet Will
I seek you everywhere
in the Forest of Arden (gone)
at Mountjoy House (gone)
St. Giles (no)

I will continue to seek out
a physical proximity
in London, soon in Stratford
but I recognize your presence
is everywhere

You are gone, I trust
to the gods, to the Muse
to the Elysian fields
to banter
and cavort

with Chaucer, Donne, Dickens
Jonson & Marlowe
with Milton & Joyce
with Sappho & Anais Nin

I pray for you
and for you
to inform me
Amen

My mind's ablaze—thoughts, images, reverberations
of the past, the pulse of life from oh-so-long-ago. I lay my
head against the hearth-flue and felt a hit of that pulse—
of blood and nurturance in the umbilicus that
connected newborn Will to Mary Arden Shakespeare
& to this moiety of earth that spins out the vast globe,
grown diminutive when a boy from Texas traveled
to a small town in Warwickshire. Hello to you,
Will Shakespeare. Well met, timbers of Arden,
so well preserved. Greetings to dust of now-
cobbled Henley Street raised in meeting boyhood
friends, then in travel by horse from London town...

Halloa, wife Anne, children Susanna, Judith... Dost watch thy 'haviors? dost grow in
strength and knowledge and wisdom? Wilt remember me, so long away? Down with
you to fetch me an apple and a bite of cheese, oh, and a cup of ale – nay, wine – and one
for your mother, though she'll like as not drink it not – whilst I do speak with her –
and then I'll bring thee out thy gifts from the city. Make haste, now! *And down they go,
all a'titter, eager to see what gewgaws their father hath brought 'em, down the selfsame steps I
did descend as a lad, but worn now, worn steps, worn home, worn Will.*

Well, then, ladywife. Difficult proposition, this our 'wedded life.' Nay, the fire of thy
flushing cheeks,... send me not basilisks from out thine eyes – though, God-a-mercy,
you're comely when you're angry, so you are. Nay, hear me out: I have contracted to
purchase New Place – a new home, a great place when I shall have restored it to its
former state – and, Anne, I am a gentleman, you a gentlewoman! See here the paper
on't, with our coat of arms...!!!

Yea, my love, I know too well, our Hamnet's gone, and nothing we may do can bring
him back. You say you think your time is gone, I say mayhap we'll get another son,
but we'll not know without you welcome me back to your bed.

The Great Gardens are all that remain of New Place, built 1483 by Sir Hugh Clopton.
WS purchased it 1597, the year after the death of his son, Hamnet. In 1756, then-owner
Rev Francis Gastrell, tired of visiting Bardolaters, cut down the mulberry tree said to
have been planted by WS. He finished demolition of the house in 1759—after which
he was run out of town.

Will Come a'Courtin'

Just saw Anne's Cottage (her folks' cottage) where trembling Will
came a'courtin', impelled by Cupid's shafte, his pulse a'poundin', his
mind awhirl with questions and with doubts: was Mr Hathaway alive
or dead? imposing or no? [of course he was;) was Anne a good match?
(not so bad... her family's substantial enow...)

*She's a mix all right – demure & proper one moment, then hot as the sun in July
and a heifer in heat. She's... religious – that's a goodly thing, innit? Can't tell
anymore, what with the way the wind of state doth ever turn. Pater's in a spot –
Papist in his bones, but Englishman loyal & true – now by law recusant. And I
am bound twixt ice & fire, poised between belief and the sour naysayer, landsman
caught twixt air & water, neither place a standing ground.*

*But is she a good match? Aye, if my loins answer. Hath she a modesty, too?
Aye, at war with her loins. Is she a bright lass? Aye, bright, but not for
outshining – no beacon she, but clear & clean as a spring, with a high colour
to match her copper hair. Well, then, she's fair enow, and bright and spirited–
but a little too inclined to the new Puritan persuasion. Heigh ho!
Let time tell.*

*So, then, what then? Her mother calls, and Anne brings word, bowing low–
ohhh, her breasts, I long to touch again, and nuzzle, to inhale her scent
(and well she knows it.) Well, well, then, I'll just go in and sit at the fire
with her – and her mother. ...that's safe, innit?*

I sit beneath the only thatched roof remaining in Stratford, smoke my
pipe, sip a bitter and ruminate the centuries.

New Olde Bread

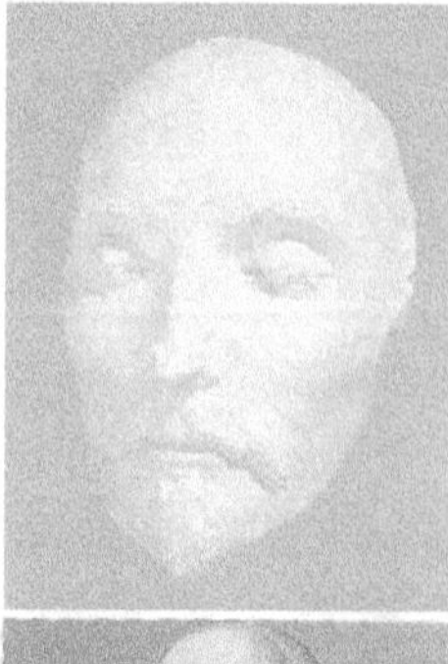

From pleasant plucking of the lute
(soft harmony from cat gut)
archaeologist of the invisible
echoing down the aedolons of history
through the longing over
home and hearth
of another when and where
        I am

resonating still in fire and air
in blood and stone
with treasure-troved ephemera
and in the threatened waters
of the Shakespeared isle
whose turning tawny
calls me back to other where
        I am

returning now to golden California
to stitch the past in present time
to bake new bread
in hearth and home
on gridlocked battlefields
where I must nock the arrow
draw and find the target
churning
            in my heart

Invocation

In expectant hush the priest ascends
the steps, brandishes the knife
to initiate the ceremony

The dithyramb begins, song of sacrifice
then in the glint of focused light
down comes the sacred blade

and in blood the price of pain is paid.

The ritual fulfilled, call forth the deity!
Bring forth Sweet Will the Honey-tongued
Poor Will, Mad Will, All Embracing Will

Will by poseurs now Usurped
and with this sacrifice let Will return to man
to Shake the Spear at ignorance.

*Non sanz droict**, still, says he
and echoes through the centuries

*the motto on Shakespeare's coat of arms, in Old Norman French, whose
direct translation is *Not Without Right,* with an alternative translation,
possibly by implication, of *By My Own Merit.*

Hearthside Stories*

But then instruction did continue, when, late of an even, after
supper and the chores were done, when a sometime genial sire
or often gracious dam, or aunt or uncle, always worn with the
day but eftsoons warmed by the hearth, (we, all of us, at our
hand-work) when one or t'other would break into a story:

Mayhap 'twas but Uncle Aubrey *[in west country dialect, in
broad gesture & old as dirt:]* "...and the tale of the cunning
cuckoo, who leaves her egg in the nest of the warbler, then
flaps away, free as the sayin', 'free as a bird' But the warbler
is not so free, for when the cuckoo's egg doth hatch, 'tis soon
big enough to push the other eggs and brood to a fatal fall."
[Aubrey enacts a terrible but comic 'splat' to the childers.]

[Aside by Will:] And then began the awful comedy,...

[Old Aubrey, again:] "...for the cuckoo grows so quickly and
so large *(Cuc-koó! Cuc-koó!)* that the little mother warbler
(Tweet, Tweet, Tweet!,) now bereft of all her progeny and
dwarfed by the giant changeling, is so beset by its insatiable
demands for food *(Gawp!)* she well nigh disappears down
the cuckoo's throat, *[Yikes!]* ere the fledgling flies the nest."

[Back to Will:] Now, every story had a moral, and the moral
here was... *[retrieving it]*

[Aubrey:] "Look well to thy eggs ere they be hatched!"

Then there was the story of *[as aunt:]* "that saucy wife of a
distant, ancient, flinty cousin, Leofric of Mercia, which lady,
to protest mi'lord's o'er heavy taxes on the people, did ride in
stately progress on her palfrey through the town of Coventry
with naught upon her person but her flaxen locks and smile –
aye, by Jesu, Lady Godiva! A relative!" *[Will again, gleefully
kicking back in chair:]* How I did love these family tales!

Hearthside Stories is an excerpt of the play *Alms for Oblivion*

Shakespeare to a Comely Lass

I would not hurt thee, this I fain would say
When questioned toward my truest of intent:
I fain would tell thee thou must go away
Or e'er my heart, or thine, should be rent

But I have not the Will to will thee gone
For what would I without thy tender gaze
Nor must I 'low myself for thee to long
When it might mar the grace you lend the days

O let mine eye be then the window to my soul
Wherein thou seest mirror to thy worth
Who live a longing, both of us, to hold
A wholeness in each moment, yea, a birth

For I am born in every smile I see
Which, though it be on others, comes from thee!

The Grandest Show*

He sits slowly. BASIC LIGHTS BEGIN SLOW DIM.
SPECIAL UP TO HALF.

*Twas in my 11th year upon this orb of infinite discoveries,
and we had just returned from weeklong holiday of
Whitsuntide, that I did daydream on the recentest events;
Sir Robert Dudley, Earl of Leicester, had been hosting the
Virgin Queen in the grandest show of hospitality imaginable:*

He jumps up. BASIC LIGHTS BUMP UP. *He runs
circuitous route back to chair:*

Fayther, Fayther, I had shouted out
Running home from school. *Dearest Sire,*
Then leapt into his lap all eyes and flame.
*The Queen doth come anon to Kenilworth,
And there's to be great show and entertainment!
Oh, may we go? O say that we may go!
Richard Quiney and his kin will go,
And all the town. Oh, let us go with them!*
And sober man he was, and alderman,
But did consent, (excusing it as duty.)
We made the journey of some fifteen mile
Together with the Quineys. All the children
Piled into the cart were rollicking
Or bored or both, and never, ever, ever
Soon enough, but soon enough we came
To Kenilworth. Oh, the Castle looming up
Tall as a mountain, big as a bustling town,
Was decked out in the summer's finery
And welcomed Queen and all with great estate.
And the pageantry was grander than
I ever saw nor never saw again:
The evening sky did blaze with fireworks!

A handsome lake illuminate by torch
Did buoy up a giant mermaid singing
(By dint of singers couched in the machine,)
And Arion rode upon a dolphin's back
(Another huge mechanical) that swam
Up to Her Majesty upon the bridge...

*[He's assumed the heroic pose of Arion, about to speak.
Nothing comes. Still nothing.]*

He quite forgot his lines, then doffed and held
His horse's head and blurted out, *Your Grace,*
  I am not Arion, not he, but honest
  Harry Goldingham. (Or, mayhap, Bottom.)

[Sits. BASIC LIGHTS BEGIN X-FADE TO SPECIAL.]

And so I dreamed, and then in dreaming dreamt
  What if, what if, what if...?

[LIGHTS TO SPECIAL ONLY. *In broad west-country
dialect:*]

OBERON: My gentle Pucke, come hither. etc...

*Excerpt from Alms for Oblivion.

The Authorship 'Question'*

Will examines folio on table:

But what noble work is here? Is't a new rendering of Plutarch?
Belike that saucy Ovid! Let me see... *[Reads spine of book. Thrilled:]*
Z'ounds... 'tis I and mine own progeny?   *[Paging through:]*
By the Holy Rood, look you—Heminge and Condell saved my
plays and put 'em to print! **The Tempest** first? Hmm..

*[His attention arrested, evaluates a moment, then holds up frontispiece
 with Droeshout engraving. Deadpan:]*
Not the face, methinks, shall launch a thousand hearts.
The Inscription is by Ben Jonson. I'faith, good friend, dear
friends all, my deepest thanks. *[Remembering:]* Ben did tell me
later in Elysium of his charge in this, and that he — cut my plays!

[Will flips furiously through text:]   "Small Latin and less Greek"
indeed! This drinks deep; drinks cup and all...

*[Loses himself in dotage as he reads, then abruptly regards audience.
Holding up title page, again he approaches them:]*

Look you, mistress, what says the Title Page? Cans't thou read it?
 [If so, have her read aloud. If not—] Nay? Then I shall be thine eyes
and tongue, too:
  Master William Shakespeare's
  Comedies, Histories & Tragedies

Not Sir Francis Bacon's Crisps? & Soggy Prose?
  Published according to the True Originall Copies

Not deVere's devices?
  London, ... Isaac Jaggard & Edward Blount, 1623

Not the ghostly incantations of a Resurrected Marlowe?
Who, then, wrote the plays?!?

Thou, sir, I beseech thee tell us thy surname. [*Audience answer:_________*] Very well. I shall aspire for thee progenerative pow'r. Let us then say Master _________ hath 1, 2, 3, 4 children, nourished in the womb of their Mother. (Sired honestly, so the Mother tells us.) Oh, who will grudge young Mistress Mary___________ her name? Who will force on her another name? rob her of inheritance? rob her father of his progeny!?! [*Heating to the task, he begins to pace.*] Now, follow me on this, I pray ye: Old Master Shakespeare hath some 40 children—saying nought of countless little songs and sonnets running 'round. 40 children have his name upon 'em. Nourished in the womb of *pia mater*. Mothered by the Muse. What says the Mother's mouthpiece, friend and rival Jonson? [*Holds up book:*] "Shakespeare!" Midwived by some three-score players and printers. What say midwives Heminges, Condell, Jaggard, Blount? "Shakespeare!!!". But there be some must [*Slams book shut:*] meddle. [*In high dudgeon, as scholarly twit (yes, we've all seen this fellow!:)*] "Nay," say they, "let us rather doubt our eyes and ears and find inventions to deny a bumpkin boy of Warwick with none of learning—nay, nor Norman blood—could ever sire such progeny! Why, certes they were written by a University Wit, or some great Lord of Learning—mayhap the Queen herself did write 'em!" God's Teeth! Fie, say I! Fie and double-fie!! I will claim mine own as mine or either tell ye they were written by an infinite number of monkeys with an infinite number of quills!!!

*Excerpt from *Alms for Oblivion*.

When I Left Stratford Town*

When I left Stratford Town with the players the voluble part
of me did reason thus: 'twas the fittest way to find out Dame
Fortune and reconstitute the family honour! I had promised
when I left to visit often (as often as the tumbledown fortunes
of the road allowed) and to bring money. On my first visit
home with a golden angel (a 10s.piece,) Anne and I did
penetrate the ice and find our way back to the conjugal bed;
[Moving STAGE RIGHT:] and on my third visit I had sold a
play for the princely sum of £2!! *[Stops:]* 'Twas Providential,
for I found myself the father of twins: Judith and Hamnet.
I had got a son!!!

[Moves CENTER-STAGE:]
But I'd hitched my star to the players' wagon and went again in
pursuit of Mistress Fortune's pretty petticoats. Nay, there was
more: the world was bursting in me, needed out, and the
players had a way to give it voice.   Oh, 'twas a dream fulfilled
to, all unknowing, join with Leicester's men. The low man
in the barnyard, this young cock, now was Chanticleer and
cock-a-doodle all the tour and all the way to London Town!

When at last the oarsman's cry came "Eastward-Ho!" and
Burbage took me by the arm to steady my crossing of the
vasty Thames, mine eye and heart and mind were set ablaze
with sight of the Tower, the Bridge, the vault of St Paul's with
spires of smaller cathedrals round about like a mother swan
and her brood; with the din and the bustle and the size of
London life. Never mind my gorge did turn at the sight of
severed heads on London bridge, all agape for kites to peck at,
staring on oblivion; or rise again at the stench of the running
sewers in the city. 'Twas the price to pay for being at the
center of the whirling world! Queen Elizabeth was God's own
anointed — aye, and worthy, too — and her people loved her well!
Drake was soon to set to rout the Spanish monarchs of the sea,
the once invincible Armada. And England was become the

"sceptered isle." Books were plentiful, and every day new
translations and inventions and discoveries were put to print
with ever increasing speed. A largesse universal lay before us,
as a sea of possibility bounded only by the limits of imagination.

And the theatre! Oh, the theatre! No more playing from the
back of a cart; no more bull pits, no more Guild Halls, no
more country inn-yards. This was the particular place for the
playing of a play. The founder of our troupe – the fiery James
Burbage – was a man of vision, and when he built the playhouse
there was none like, so he simply called it 'The Theatre."

'Twas modeled after bear gardens, which, though ill-used for
the baiting of bears and bulls, had a most felicitous design: a
wooden 'O' did circumscribe an open pit, over a moiety of
which was thrust a stage, with three tiers for the seating of up
to two thousand auditors, of the which, together with the
groundlings standing in the pit, there was not a single pair of
ears farther from the mouth of the speaker on the stage than a
hundred feet. A noble edifice, indeed! The best; but yet
that best was bested yet again by the Globe, that Phoenix-like
was resurrected from the timbers of her mother...
[Stops short.] I like that.
[Hurries to table, seizing book and quill in inkwell. SITS to write:]

"...that Phoenix-like was resurrected from the timbers..."—
hmm....'ashes'?—nay, 'timbers' is the better choice...

[Finds inkwell dry.]
'Tis gone dry. Well, then, 'tis gone.

[Pensive, he eases folio shut]

*Excerpt from Alms for Oblivion.

A Silken Kiss

This love is not a Harlequin Romance,
no smooth fit, nor yet perfect fantasy
of untrammeled conjugal ecstasy,
but a miracle to which we've grown by chance.
The universe is redolent with chaos
that can freeze our blood or shake the earth,
and in the most mysterious ways it births
invisible order from agape and eros.
For somehow in this spinning happenstance
we chafe the burrs and edges of the past,
release their lease to let the present last,
because we've learned our molecules will dance.

And such a wild and wondrous dervish dance as this
we found with but a searching, longing, silken kiss!

Dark Lady Sonnet 1.

One self, my soul, that self in me that's bold,
Doth tell me that my love for thee is true,
My heart is strong, my fragile frame can hold
The power of this flame that burns me through.
The other self, my heart, that self that fears,
Doth warn me with remembrance of pain,
Of loves long lost, of lost love's bitter tears –
I fain would flee that story told again.
But yet myself doth say thyself is true,
The while one self the other holds at rout,
For thou, my soul, my heart, my blazoned hue
Of love, doth counsel all my selves to doubt:

That she that hath my single self, my all,
Now keeps her tender heart behind a wall.

Dark Lady Sonnet 2.

Oh, do I play the fond and prating fool
For that I drink so deeply of thine eyes,
That when I plunge me in their almond pool
I certain am that I have claimed the prize
Beyond all reckoning? And when I sup
The honeyed chalice of thy op'ning lips
And swim the flood that overflows thy cup
To goddess blossom couched between thy hips,
I bow before thine altar, thou to mine
Dost open up in reverence thy gate
That, we, in mingling essences, divine
A higher state that's transubstantiate.

But this my fondest dream of alchemy:
I would grow daily old and young with thee.

Dark Lady Sonnet 3.

There is a she whom thou, my heart would know
Beyond the meeting of our passion's swell,
Beneath the visage which she 'lows to show
And for whose love wouldst follow into hell.
There is a she who conjures thee to praise,
In words of poesy, of wonders kind,
And, basking in this poet's roundelays,
Begets a wonder in this wand'ring mind;
For whilst she smiles and coos at tender touch,
Is tender, too, and kind, and seeks to please,
That sacred, secret soul thou lov'st so much
Now stakes herself behind her boundaries.

She thereby adds sad measure of my gain
That, thus awarding pleasure, grants me pain.

The Playing of Plays*

The playing of plays proved difficult with the plague and the good puritans of London Council. From one pulpit the matter was argued thus *[LEANS OVER BACK OF CHAIR. AS FIRE & BRIMSTONE MINISTER:]* "The cause of plagues is sin; the cause of sin is plays; argal, if you look to it well, the cause of plagues is plays!" Scintillating logic, eh? Well nigh might have prevailed had not Her Majesty wanted to hear plays. God Save The Queen!!! [X.D.C:] Even still, the theatres must needs be shut in summer months when plague was at its worst; and on our return the bawdy houses reeked of the pox. Kit Marlowe, the great rapscallion of the stage, he whose chiefest pleasures were said to be tobacco and boys, lately of Her Majesty's secret service and one who would not hold his tongue—why, this same Christopher Marlowe (now, think on't, I the coming rival!)—was sent to silence, stabbed in the eye and slain in a hugger-mugger tavern brawl in Deptford.

On kai me`on; farewell!

Farewell, indeed, O thou comet! Hahh! *On kai me`on.* There was a dainty jewel of a phrase for him to couch in *Dr. Faustus.* Greek to me. Greek to all and everyone. I had forgot the 'little Greek' I'd learnt and snagged Kit in the Mermaid afterwards to ask its meaning; at the which he feigned surprise, then disappointment, then fixed me with his stare as the hawk will eye the sparrow and with a patience born of conspiratorial urgency whispered *Being and not being, Will: pure ontology. To be or not to be!* That... was the <u>answer</u>!

*Excerpt from *Alms For Oblivion.* I would like to thank and acknowledge DJ Carlile, who, for the entirety of the time I was at Faire as William Shakespeare, admirably embodied the role of Christopher Marlowe. He it was who pointed out to me the meaning of *On kai me`on..*

Tomorrow

is Sweet Willie's birthday
and I merely wanting to celebrate
put out the word
sheaves of mailed missives
tossed into the dark and
        soundless

no not of impact
nor yet no mangos shipped
no echo in the emptiness
nor even a stray crab apple
hey – all in a day's life's
        bitter harvest

So   What?
Let's suck the lemon
with a chunk of honeycomb
and at the bidding of the bee
larva, plant a seed
        of mirth

Eh   What say'st thou
to a goodly jest? – buzz!
buzz! – a mirthful jest?
a laugh at scars
in knowing wounds
        can heal

Author's Note: This bit of existential angst arose out of an effort to find funding for the play I was writing in fits and starts, but which I eventually had to produce myself. I elected to appear at the open mic at the Comedy Store on Shakespeare's birthday (April 23) to work out my opening material in the play that became *Alms for Oblivion*. I was invited back, but I opted not to get into that comic rut, pandering for laughs. I was determined to trust the material I was writing.

A Feast of Languages Speech

(Will's 427th Birthday Party Fundraiser for the Globe Rebuilding Project)

It is a matter of no small amaze to me that I do find myself here. Had I the capacity to conceive as a youth that I would one day celebrate (with others) the occasion of my 427th Natal Day... I should have made a great poet.

But this, dear my friends, is the happy destination of no easy journey. Imagine, if you will, lounging with Anäis Nin at the font of Thespis, basking in the erotic poesy of centuries, when, summoned by the Muse, I was willy-nilly plucked from Paradise and plunged into a place someone did call West Wood. (How unlike the woods of my youth!)

I'sooth, there was about the place a martial air – knives flashing about, juggled by a fellow with 8 fingers. You know they're sharp, madam!

Upon asking directions hither, I was told by a young fellow, "Dude, speak English!"

Thus, that am I summoned to a Feast of Languages is most appropriate, not the least of reasons that I did in mine own time appropriate the polyphony of many tongues in one, the progeny of many warring forebears: Picts, Angles, Celts, Romans, Saxons, Danes, Normans. We have, 'twould seem, been willing, even as we killed one another, to appropriate the livingness of languages.

Thus am I most proud that I— who once had the
audacity to strive to cram into our little wooden-O all
the world, from sceptered isle to Trojan shore, and, yea,
beyond into uncharted islands on the vasty seas— that I
should now hear our progeny turned to the tongues of
all Illyrias, and the great globe itself grown like unto our
little Globe of ages past, soon, God willing, of ages
present and ages yet to come.

To you, dear friends, and those you represent, that I
may now bask in the fulfillment of this task, my
heartfelt and everlasting thanks.

I leave you now with but one remonstrance, a riddle, if
you will: as the world doth smaller grow and becomes
endangered by our presence, theatre must the greater
grow.

Well met!

*Faire Favour**

*A fest indeed, O noble sentiment
To honour me at suche a banquet table.
O wondrous tyme, to have this merriment
With suche deare friends and lovers – it were fable!
Stories, then? Aye, bawdy tales, and yet
Something more is up than that we toast.
Why, tales of Roll-me-over-Juliet?
It doth appear to me you've planned a roast.
Aroint! Was't Bacon, then, that writ that song?
Why, that great ham can hoist the flagge!
Love-apple Jonson? When all is said and Donne,
Set on by Mother Rose and Father Stagge!
But, grammercy, suche spirits there ensued
Methinks I was not roasted, then, but stewed!*

*Then try me thus with importunity
I'll vow, should come the opportunity:
Yea, spyce me as ye will with wit and savour,
When called, Dear Friends, I shall return the favour.*

*Ye Rose & Stag, Blackpoint, Novato

The Three Graces

So now the Festival is o'er and done,
We did our deeds upon the field of play,
We've wrangled and we've reveled, every one,
And said so much, yet one thing left to say:
O there be stalwarts in the world of Faire
And in the nurturance of growing minds,
But there be some for whom we are aware
The trumpet must be sounded to the winds:
Oh, yea, to goodwives Karin, Pam and Nan
Let countless coats of arms festoon the wall,
And let the dragon dance to pipes of Pan
For ye who laboured for the good of all.

For ye this flow'r, this scroll, this testament
To loving hearts with loving thanks are sent.

Lost Sonnet

*That you are mother to my son befriends
the meaning of the world's nativity,
betokens hope for what the future sends
and lends a blessing to eternity;
and this derives a grace for youth well spent
in lease of Time's accrued prosperity,
nor any capable to circumvent
but lays the debt on our posterity.*

*This you do know, but do you know as well
your mother had a daughter, she a jewel
beyond the ken of aught that I can tell?
Tis she that o'er my heart did once hold rule
a she that once was fair, and kind, and true*

That she is she I tell myself is you.

Mothering Day

Down through the many centuries now past
We've sought to honor pow'rful cosmic forces,
Embodiments of qualities that last
The ages—gods, belike, who shape our courses.
Now, this day do we call Mothering Day.
Then let John Barleycorn and Zeus abide,
For we shall honor goddesses today
And let the fathers wait for time betide.
So do we honor Gaia and Cybele?
Yea, but yet, the goddess, I aver:
'Twas a woman bred thee, bore thee, birthed thee
And tendered thee, O let us honor her!

Tell me this, my sisters and my brothers,
Where would we all be without our mothers?

Friday the 13th*

CHORUS
In honor of this most auspicious day
I've summoned up a coven convocation
For 'tis a Friday, and 13th, of May—
Darkling spirits at their dim vocation.
And though the title's feared, I still can say
Here's a weird or three from the Scottish Play:

1st Witch: When shall we three meet again
                    In thunder, lightning, or in rain?
2nd Witch: When the hurlyburly's done,
                    When the battle's lost and won.
3rd Witch: That will be ere the set of sun.
1st Witch: Where the place?
2nd Witch: Upon the heath.

*   *   *

1st Witch: Look what I have.
2nd Witch: Show me, show me.
1st Witch: Here I have a pilot's thumb,
                    Wreck'd as homeward he did come.
[Drum within]
3rd Witch: A drum, a drum!
                    Macbeth doth come.

ALL
The weird sisters, hand in hand,
Posters of the sea and land,
Thus do go about, about:
Thrice to thine and thrice to mine

And thrice again, to make up nine.
Peace! the charm's wound up.

[Enter MACBETH and BANQUO]

MACBETH
So foul and fair a day I have not seen.

CHORUS
And thus the bearded Muse doth paint upon
The heath her tale of Power, darkly drawn
From bleak palette that lacks the color of the heart,
But contraries have their balances,
And every tail, methinks, must have a head:

DON PEDRO
How, how, pray you? You amaze me: I would have
thought her spirit had been invincible against all
assaults of affection.

BEATRICE
By my troth, I am sick.

MARGARET
Get you some of this distilled Carduus Benedictus,
and lay it to your heart: it is the only thing for a qualm.

CHORUS
'Tis thus the light will seek out darknesses
And thus each blue may have for balm its red.

* This is some quickly assembled little Mummer's frivolity at Faire.

Wake

So now she's gone, and nothing we may say
Can bring her back, except by recollection.
I trust our thoughts may send her on her way
Yet keep her always dear in our reflection.
Where be those lips that you before had kissed
And found a love that stayed through weal or woe?
Where be the hand whose touch is sorely missed,
The Dam of strength that Time must overflow?
Though yet this dullish substance be consigned
To well-earned rest and mingle with the soil,
The mortal theft displayed is but a sign
Of spirit 'scaped from misery and toil.
Take heart, my dears, as I who mourn with you,
And joy in she, interred, that's borne anew!

The Wheels of the Gods

'Tis said the wheels of the gods slowly grind
Upon the tapestry we mortals weave,
Who, ever harried chapman lackeys, find
Our grain is ground to dust upon Time's sleeve.
For, truly, painful labours topple still,
Oaths on gilded monuments foresworn,
The whilst we plant and water, reap and till
And mumble curses 'gainst oblivion.
So yet we strive and strive the livelong while
To keep our grapes from rotting on the vine,
Forgetful still, bereft still, of the smile
That knows the noble sacrifice for wine:

Aye, grist for the mill or grapes for the press, if true,
Then happy, I, to be such wine with you!

Kaleidoscope

I am … not as I appear to be
for though no other than I am
mayhap (methinks)
you hearing, seeing
think me other than yourself
yet I am you, you see?

For I am merely mirror to your being
here reflecting beauty of your body
your suppleness of thigh
pattern of your breath through parted lips
mosaics of your eyes before and after they are lit
and colors of surprises

    I am weaver
    spinning out the visions
    of the dreams we hear

        Shhhhhsh! Quiet!
        Shuuuush the mind!
        Shhhhhhhhsh!

I am poet

I am you

raining words to aim a thought

and paint an image wrought of

  dancing Pan with pipe at dawn

  bloody meat

  dirty streets

  indulgence in despair

  falling, falling into rising here

rising into ever-incandescent lamp of love

  birthing tendrils of this greening breath of earth

  with dervish dance upon the lake

rising in Apollo's chariot at noon

  into the secret sweet eternally celestial song

    and angels' wings by moonlight

What, you may ask, is this poem doing in the context of my quest for WS?
I wrote this poem after hours in the dim star-and-candle-light @ Don
 Brown's tea & coffee emporium, which was called at the time, Mullah's, I
believe. This would be before it was changed to Nasrudin's Donkey. So,
yes, dear reader, dear afficionado, it is very much a poetical (if you so deem it)
work of faire, and thus a part of the quest. If the title is a 19th Century word –
well, then, so be it. 'Twas after all, after hours!

Dance of Endings & Beginnings

What is this dance that weaves
its way amid our revelries
amid the pennants jubilant
waving in the evening breeze?

As golden lads and lasses prance
& sing & laugh & leap & peer
in youth's abrupt exuberance
to ring the springing of the year

With nary a care nor fear
'Tis theirs to choose
      La Danse Joyeuse

What is that drone of melody
that whispers through the trees
and cuts in ancient counterpoint
our major joys in minor keys?

As queen and dashing courtier
lady, lord, burgher, barkeep
the ploughman and the warrior—
all—lay plans to sow and reap

Reapers o'er the landscape creep
and Time turns the knob
        La Danse Macabre

Grand ringout now is drawing nigh
but waxing as our sun is spent
the moon doth our attention try
and we gaze on in wonderment

The sun we see is in eclipse
and yet is left penumbral haze
as moon doth mask in her ellipse
to light our way to future days

of faires to come and faires to pass
renewal of the cov'ring grass

Sceptre, learning, physic must
*All follow this and come to dust**

        La Danse Macabre?
        La Danse Joyeuse!

                Faire's End, 2012
            *Shakespeare's **Cymbeline***

The Green Man Inn

I find me lost in dreams of Faire at night,
Lights out, the screams of revelry abate,
But yet, where none before, there's candlelight
Ahead, a burning brazier at the gate
So long familiar—it's the Green Man Inn.
*I stand and muse, **How like a fairy ring!***
Until a hand doth reach to let me in

I pause to list: ethereal voices softly sing—

It's Indus sets a gentle rippling in the air!
There's Kage, she's radiant, no Mother Bumby by
There's Kent, resplendent ever, and Burbage Neil is there
And Kevin Brown regales, and bosoms all are high
Ron Patterson in motley tells a saucy tale
While Phyllis smiles softly, lets out a tender sigh
Tim raises up his tankard in praise of flowing ale
Mark Lewis paints word pictures, summons visions nigh

I go to seat myself, yet Kage turns me away:
"There's Time enough," she smiles
> *"and you've much left to say."*
My longing speaks my part, "But ye are kith and kin!"
"When comes the Time, Dear Heart, there's room
> *at the Green Man Inn."*

'Til Journey's End

O! on such full and glorious days as these
When heaven's master orb doth gaily smile
The banners out and laughing in the breeze
Flung into a dance to play the while,
Such days when I have dallied with a lover
And splashed in careless immortality
(In present world's fountain or another)
In union's grace known no frugality—
E'en still, I've wandered back to mem'ries bleak
When region clouds did mask our Father Sun,
When winter's chill hath made my fire seem weak,
And I, in search of sweet relief, found none

If love you'd have, my love, till journey's end,
I'll not be reckoned as 'faire weather friend.'

www.ingramcontent.com/pod-product-compliance
Lightning Source LLC
Chambersburg PA
CBHW071508030726
47593CB00003B/1211